PAPER CRANE

PAN
NER

The traditional Japanese paper crane or *orizuru* is famous throughout the world. It is a symbol of origami and a symbol of peace. An ancient Japanese legend says that whoever folds 1000 cranes will be granted a wish.

Today, in Hiroshima, stands the peace memorial of Sadako Sasaki built by her classmates in her memory to inspire peace around the world. Sadako was a victim of atom-bomb disease and she folded cranes until she died. She never gave up on her wish to be well.

1

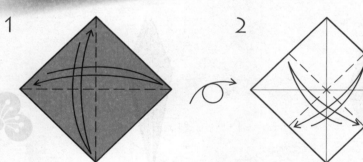

Start coloured side up.
Fold and unfold diagonals. Turn over.

2

Book fold and unfold.

3

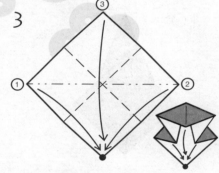

Bring three corners down to meet bottom corner. Start with corners 1 and 2 together followed by corner 3.

4

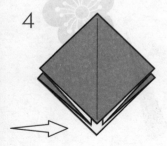

Completed preliminary base.

5

Fold top layer to the centre crease.

6

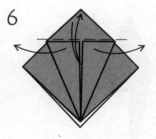

Fold and unfold the top triangle down.
Unfold flaps.

1

MODEL: TRADITIONAL, JAPAN
DIAGRAM: MATTHEW GARDINER

7

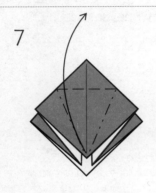

Lift the top layer upwards.

8

Step 7 in progress, the model is 3D. Fold the top layer inwards on existing creases.

9

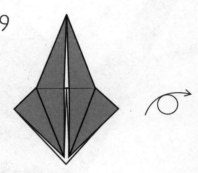

Step 7 completed, the model will be flat. Turn over.

10

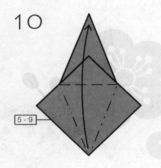

Repeat steps 5-9 on this side.

11

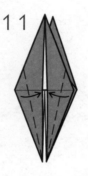

Narrow the bottom points on the top layer only. Repeat behind.

12

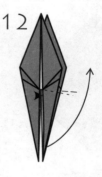

Reverse fold the bottom point upwards.

13

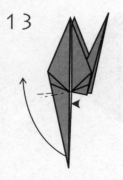

Your model should look like this. Repeat on the other side.

14

Completed body. The next steps focus on the head.

15

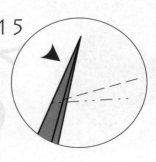

Reverse fold the point to create the head.

16

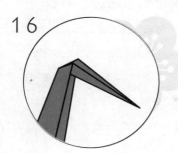

Head completed.

17

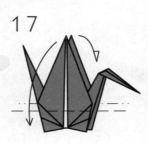

Fold wings down.

18

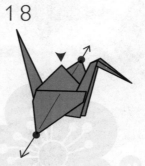

Pull the wings gently to shape the body.

19

Completed paper crane – repeat 1000 times for a wish.

SENBAZURU

MODEL: TRADITIONAL, JAPAN
DIAGRAM: MATTHEW GARDINER

Senbazuru is a Japanese word that literally means 1000 cranes. One of the world's oldest known origami books, *Hiden Senbazuru Orikata*, reveals the secrets of folding senbazuru origami. This technique requires specific cuts in the paper, that create multiple squares that are joined by small areas of paper. This technique requires a high degree of patience and skill, so take your time when folding, and be prepared to make many attempts.

A special note.

These diagrams differ to the other diagrams in this book; in that you are not shown every step of the way. You are encouraged to discover your own way.

First learn how to fold a paper crane from memory, and then become familiar with the parts of the crane; the wings, the tail and the head. Study where these parts originate on the unfolded sheet.

Once you have this familiarity, the folding of the cranes in the correct location will not be too difficult.

The difficult part is not tearing the paper connections while you are folding. More paper between the cuts will provide additional strength, so leave more paper rather than less when cutting, and then refine the cuts when the model is folded.

These diagrams have two special symbols.

The location of cuts as red lines.

The location of the head of each crane is marked as a small circle.

1A

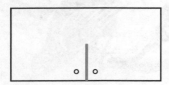

Joined at the wing. 2:1 rectangle.

1B

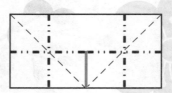

Place these creases, then cut on red line.

1C

Joined at the wing.

2A

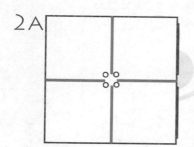

4 Kissing cranes.
1:1 square.

2B

Fold into quarters, make the creases as shown, then cut on red lines.

2C

Fold carefully to keep the cranes still kissing.

3A

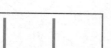

3 in a row.
3:1 rectangle.

3B

Fold into thirds, make creases as shown, then cut on red lines.

3C

These cranes are joined tail to wing. Can you make a longer chain?

4A

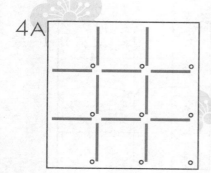

3 squared.
1:1 Square.

4B

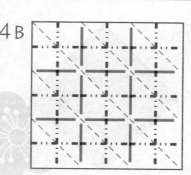

Fold into thirds. make creases as shown, then cut on red lines.

4C

This beautiful model is worth the time it takes to master.

BUTTERFLY

MODEL: TRADITIONAL, JAPAN
DIAGRAM: MATTHEW GARDINER

Butterflies capture the imagination of children and adults alike. Their delicate shape is perfect for hanging decorations. Try using a patterned sheet of origami paper.

This butterfly is a traditional fold from Japan.

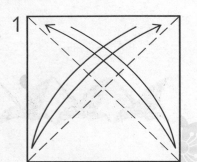

Fold and unfold diagonals.

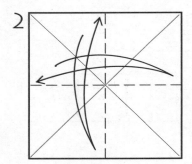

Book fold.

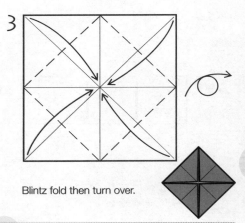

Blintz fold then turn over.

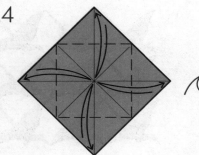

Blintz fold then turn over.

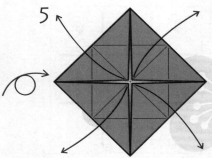

Completely unfold out to a flat sheet.

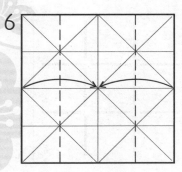

Fold sides to the middle.

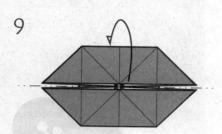

7

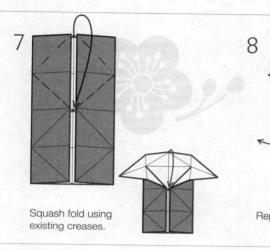

Squash fold using
existing creases.

8

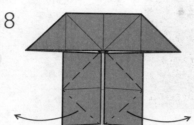

Repeat step 7 on the bottom.

9

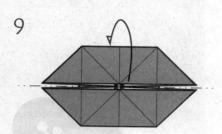

Mountain fold in half.

10

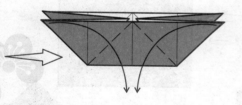

Fold points on the top layer down.

11

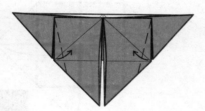

Fold sides in.

12

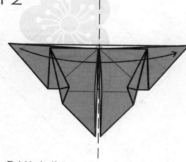

Fold in half.

13

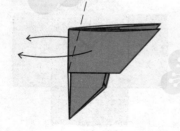

Fold both wings.

14

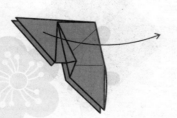

Fold one wing back.

15

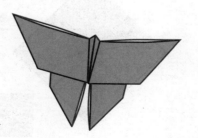

Completed butterfly.

YAKKO-SAN

MODEL: TRADITIONAL, JAPAN
DIAGRAM: MATTHEW GARDINER

Yakko-san is a very old, very well-known traditional origami form. It originates from the era of the samurai. Yakko-san comes from the word *Yatsuko* meaning servant. Yakko-san was the man carrying the baggage for his master. In contemporary Japanese society, Yakko-san has come to mean "young man".

Yakko-san is a popular design in Japanese kimono prints.

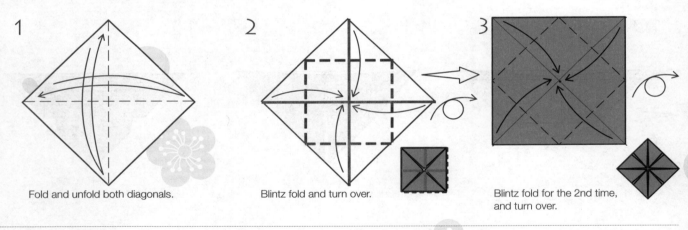

1 Fold and unfold both diagonals.

2 Blintz fold and turn over.

3 Blintz fold for the 2nd time, and turn over.

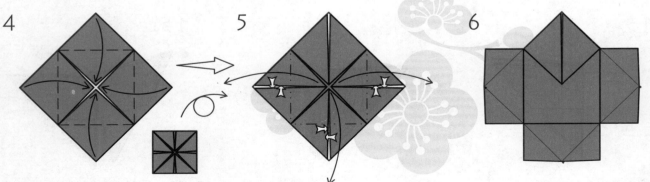

4 Blintz fold and turn over for the 3rd time.

5 Squash fold the three corners as shown. The corners will open outwards and form the square arms and feet.

6 Completed Yakko-san, konnichi-wa.

SAMURAI HELMET

MODEL: TRADITIONAL, JAPAN
DIAGRAM: MATTHEW GARDINER

The samurai helmet, or *kabuto* can be made from a large square of paper and be worn as a paper warrior's hat.

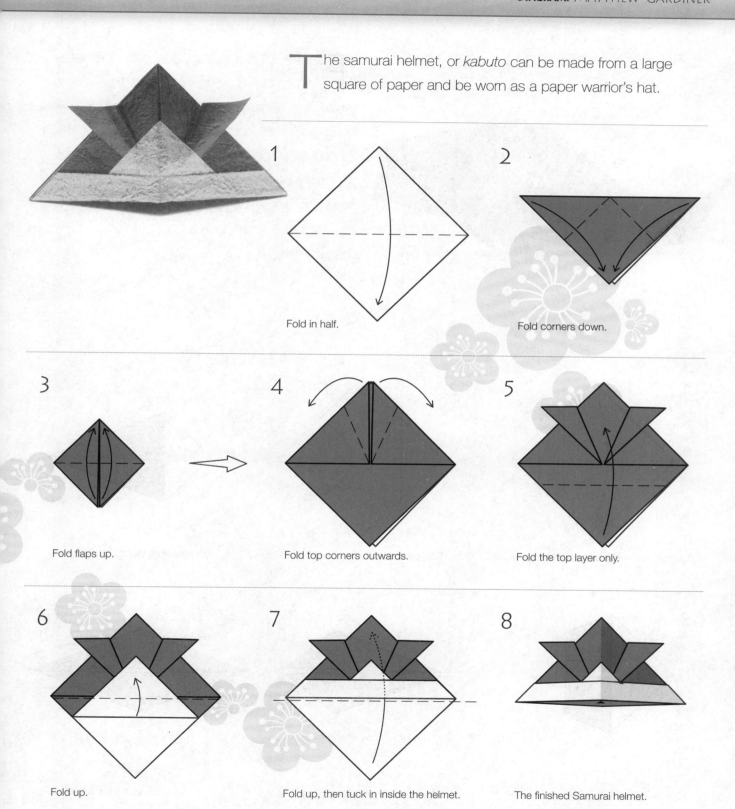

1

Fold in half.

2

Fold corners down.

3

Fold flaps up.

4

Fold top corners outwards.

5

Fold the top layer only.

6

Fold up.

7

Fold up, then tuck in inside the helmet.

8

The finished Samurai helmet.

9

FISH

MODEL: TRADITIONAL, JAPAN
DIAGRAM: MATTHEW GARDINER

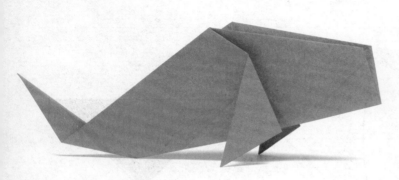

Fish are adored by the Japanese, both as a food and as a symbol of health, vitality and energy. A Japanese annual festival for boys uses the highly spirited carp (koi) as a symbol for energy and power. Look above the rooftops in late April to early May in Japan and you will see paper and cloth fish flying high. One fish per boy in the household is flown. Use a bright colour for this origami fish.

1

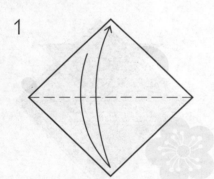

Start with white side up. Fold and unfold diagonal.

2

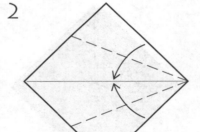

Fold both sides to the middle.

3

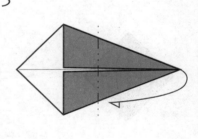

Mountain fold in half behind.

4

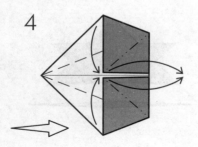

Squash fold both sides.

5

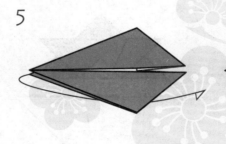

Mountain fold the back layer behind.

6

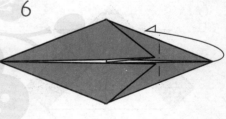

This is known as the fish base. Mountain fold the point.

7

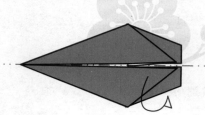

Mountain fold in half behind.

8

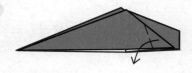

Fold the fins down on both sides.

9

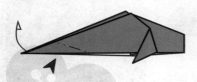

Inside reverse fold the tail.

10

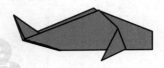

Completed fish.

KIMONO

MODEL: TRADITIONAL, JAPAN
DIAGRAM: MATTHEW GARDINER

Kimono actually means ki (wearing) and mono (thing), however in modern Japan it now describes a particular kind of customary Japanese clothing. Worn by both men and women, kimonos are nowadays mostly worn during formal events, such as marriage. The fabric of a kimono is often expensive beyond reckoning due to the intricate designs sewn with silken threads. Choose a fine patterned sheet of chiyogami or yuzen for this traditional model.

This design can be used to make a kimono for a paper doll.

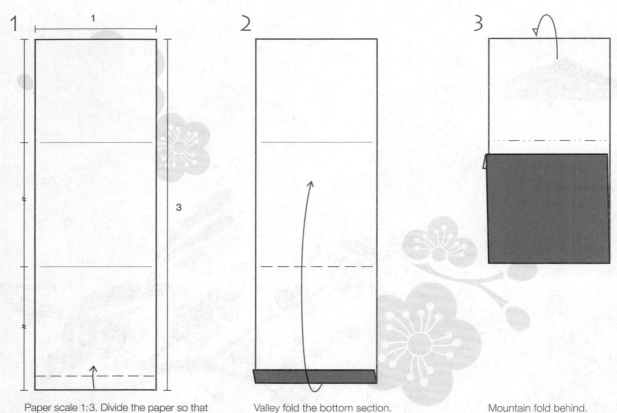

1

Paper scale 1:3. Divide the paper so that the two bottom sections are the same height and the top section is smaller. Valley fold a small flap at the bottom.

2

Valley fold the bottom section.

3

Mountain fold behind.

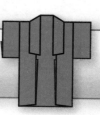

4

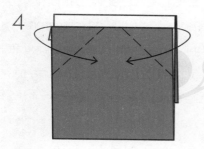

Fold the two top corners inwards.

5

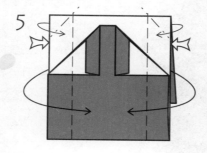

Squash fold both sides, through the top layers.

6

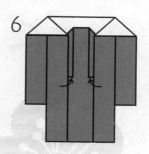

Tuck the front layer underneath the lower layer.

7

Your model should look like this. Turn over.

8

Fold down.

9

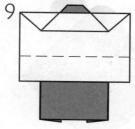

Fold upwards, creating the height of the kimono sleeves.

10

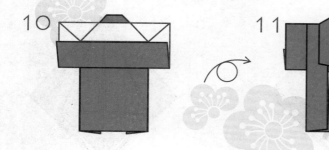

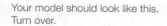

Your model should look like this. Turn over.

11

Completed kimono.

TATO

MODEL: TRADITIONAL, JAPAN
DIAGRAM: MATTHEW GARDINER

The tato is a form of paper purse or puzzle in Japan. Tatogami is a folded paper that is used to store expensive kimonos, however this tato design is for smaller objects. Origami masters Shuzo Fujimoto and Michio Uchiyama are renowned for their innovation in expanding tato designs. The primary method involves dividing the square radially, in this case into eight segments, that fold inward over each other.

Tato can be folded from fabric, or two laminated sheets of paper for maximum durability and effect.

1

Start coloured side up.
Fold and unfold diagonals. Turn over.

2

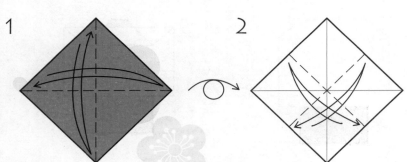

Book fold and unfold.

3

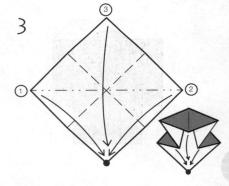

Collapse into the preliminary base.

4

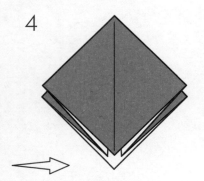

The preliminary base.

5

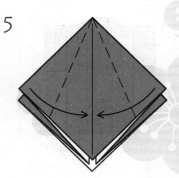

Fold edges of top layer to the centre.

6

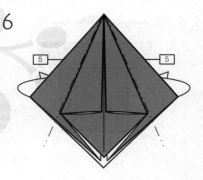

Repeat step 5 on the other side.

7

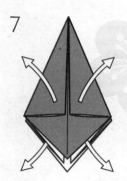

Unfold to a flat sheet.

8

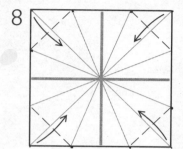

Fold corners in at the intersection of existing creases. This makes a perfect octagon.

9

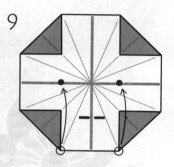

Fold the edge to the middle. Be careful to only crease as shown.

10

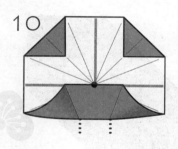

Step 9 in process. Only crease between the dotted lines.

11

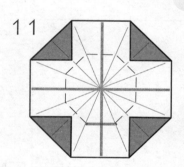

Repeat step 9 all around the octagon.

12

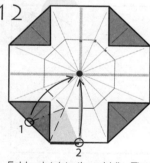

Fold point 1 to the middle. Then fold point 2. This will create a point with the greyed-out paper. Fold this point to the left. Look ahead to step 13, to see the result.

13

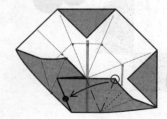

Fold the point marked by the circle to the point marked by the dot.

14

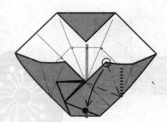

Repeat step 13 on the remaining points. The last point needs to be tucked under the first point.

15

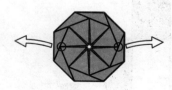

The finished tato. To open the purse gently pull on two opposite points.

WINDMILL

MODEL: TRADITIONAL, JAPAN
DIAGRAM: MATTHEW GARDINER

Windmills are iconic in the Netherlands where they harness the power of the wind for grinding grain and carving wood. This little windmill can harness the power of your breath when combined with a drawing pin and chopstick. A gentle breeze will have this model in a spin.

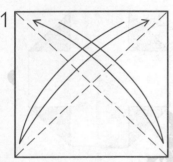

1 Fold and unfold diagonals.

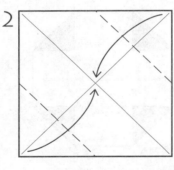

2 Half blintz fold and unfold. Turn over.

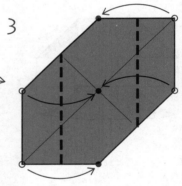

3 Fold and unfold in half.

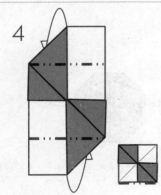

4 Mountain fold bottom and top edges to the centre. Turn over.

5 Pull out the paper from the middle.

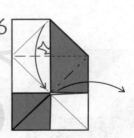

6 Squash fold, bringing the top centre corners outwards.

7

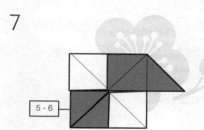

5 - 6

Repeat steps 5-6 on the bottom right corner.

8

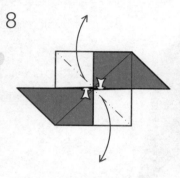

Squash fold the remaining corners outwards.

9

Completed windmill.

10

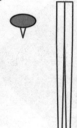

Take a drawing pin and wooden chopstick or pencil.

11

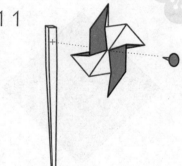

Push the pin through the centre of the windmill and into the chopstick.

12

Blow gently to make the windmill spin.

PAJARITO

MODEL: TRADITIONAL, SPAIN
DIAGRAM: MATTHEW GARDINER

Pajarito, or "Little Bird" is the most famous traditional design from Spain. Historically, Spanish origami was born from the geometric fascination of the Moors. The model requires a 3D transformation move at the end. Be careful when folding to make sure the mountain and valley folds are placed correctly. Then the final move will be almost "natural" for the paper.

The pajarito is the icon of Spanish origami. Papiroflexia is the Spanish way of saying paper folding.

1

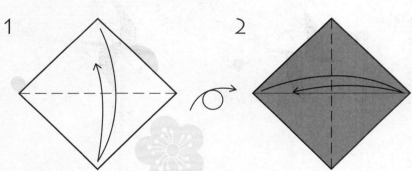

Begin white side up.
Fold and unfold diagonal. Turn over.

2

Fold and unfold diagonal.

3

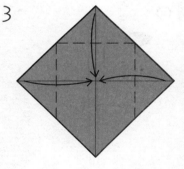

Fold three corners to the centre.

4

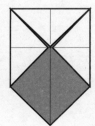

Completed step 3.
Turn over.

5

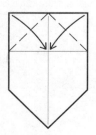

Fold top corners down to centre point.

6

Fold and unfold, be careful to only crease as shown.

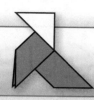

7

Unfold corners and side flaps.
Turn over.

8

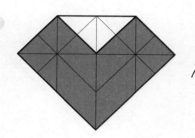

Your model should look like this.
Turn over.

9

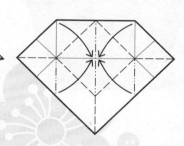

Fold on existing creases. Pay attention
to the mountain and valley folds.

10

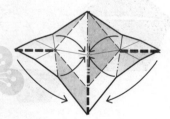

The 3D move in progress.

11

Completed pajarito.

CUP

The cup is a traditional model that actually works.

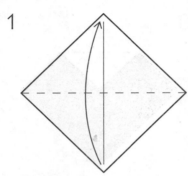

1

Fold diagonally.

2

Fold corner to side. Notice that the top edge of the fold will end up parallel to the bottom edge.

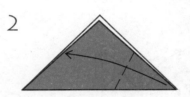

3

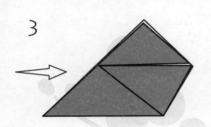

It should look like this. Turn over.

4

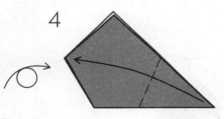

Repeat step 2 on the other side.

5

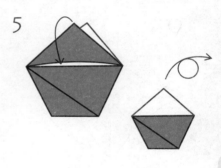

Slip top corner into pocket. Turn over.

6

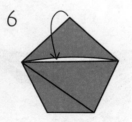

Repeat step 5 with the remaining point.

7

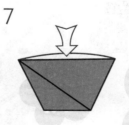

Open up pocket.

8

Completed cup.

SWAN

MODEL: TRADITIONAL, JAPAN
DIAGRAM: MATTHEW GARDINER

This simple origami swan expresses the form of this elegant bird swimming on the water of a lake.

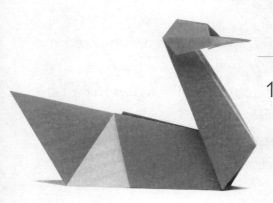

1

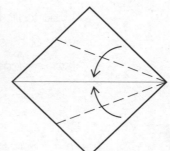

Pre-crease diagonal. Fold sides to the middle.

2

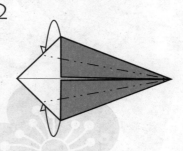

Mountain fold both sides to the middle.

3

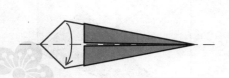

Fold in half.

4

Outside reverse fold the neck.

5

Outside reverse fold the head.

6

Pull out hidden paper on both sides of the head.

7

Pleat, then double reverse fold the head to form the beak.

8

Completed swan.

MENKO

MODEL: TRADITIONAL, JAPAN
DIAGRAM: MATTHEW GARDINER

Menko is a Japanese game that is played by two or more players with thick cards. A player's card is placed on a hardwood or concrete floor and the other player throws down their card, trying to flip the other player's card with a gust of wind or by striking their card against the other card. If they succeed, they take both cards. The player who collects the most cards wins.

This design can also be used in the household as a decorative coaster. Use chiyogami, and apply a coat or two of laquer to transform the menko into a useful item.

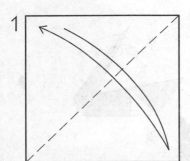

1

Fold diagonally then unfold.

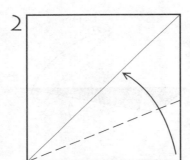

2

Fold bottom edge to diagonal crease.

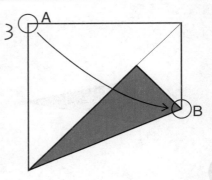

3

Fold point A to point B. Make a small crease at top.

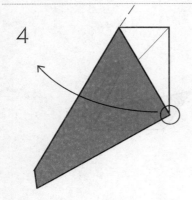

4

Where the crease touches the top edge is one third.

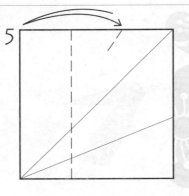

5

Fold and unfold the side edge to meet the third.

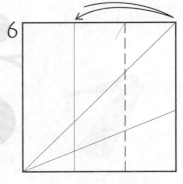

6

Fold the other edge to meet fold from step 5.

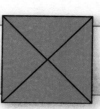

7

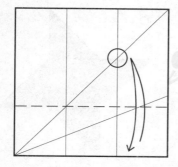

Fold the bottom edge to meet the marked intersection then unfold.

8

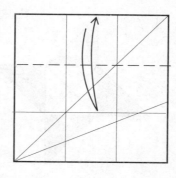

Fold and unfold top edge to meet fold from step 7.

9

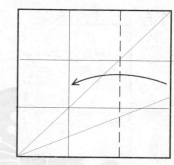

Fold in.

10

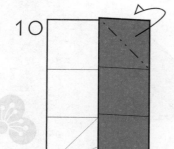

Mountain fold behind.

11

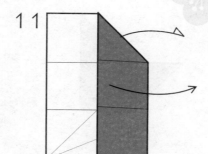

Unfold corner and open up the sheet.

12

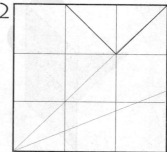

Completed steps 9-11.

13

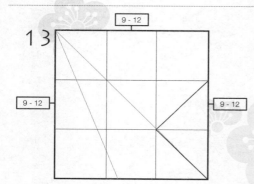

Turn the model 90°. Repeat steps 9-12 on the three remaining sides.

14

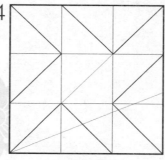

Completed crease pattern.

15

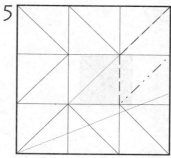

Assembly. Make the first folds as shown.

MENKO

MODEL: TRADITIONAL, JAPAN
DIAGRAM: MATTHEW GARDINER

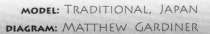

16

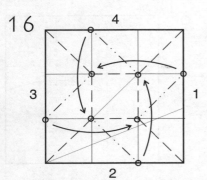

Repeat step 15 on side 2, then 3, then with 4. The last side needs to be woven to sit flat.

17

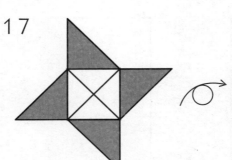

It will look like a pinwheel. Turn over.

18

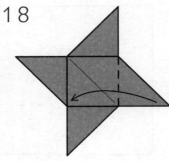

Fold point along existing crease.

19

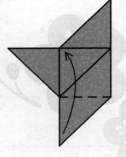

Fold the next point on top of the last.

20

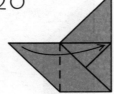

Again...

21

Fold the last point, then unfold and tuck it under the first point to lock the menko.

22

Completed menko.